About the Author

I've been told I'm many things, but going back to the roots, I know one thing is for certain, I've always been a writer. Ever since I was a young girl, I always felt the most at peace with a pen and notebook in my hand. Aside from writing, I also produce music and work full time in the medical field. I'm very blessed to have so many wonderful things on my side.

Pieces Of Us

Brittany Morgan

Pieces Of Us

Olympia Publishers
London

www.olympiapublishers.com
OLYMPIA PAPERBACK EDITION

Copyright © Brittany Morgan 2023

The right of Brittany Morgan to be identified as author of
this work has been asserted in accordance with sections 77 and 78 of
the Copyright, Designs and Patents Act 1988.

All Rights Reserved

No reproduction, copy or transmission of this publication
may be made without written permission.
No paragraph of this publication may be reproduced,
copied or transmitted save with the written permission of the publisher,
or in accordance with the provisions
of the Copyright Act 1956 (as amended).

Any person who commits any unauthorised act in relation to
this publication may be liable to criminal
prosecution and civil claims for damage.

A CIP catalogue record for this title is
available from the British Library.

ISBN: 978-1-80074-919-1

This is a work of fiction.
Names, characters, places and incidents originate from the writer's
imagination. Any resemblance to actual persons, living or dead, is
purely coincidental.

First Published in 2023

Olympia Publishers
Tallis House
2 Tallis Street
London
EC4Y 0AB

Printed in Great Britain

Dedication

I dedicate this book to my mother, whom even in her death, has helped me find my voice, find peace, and find love.

Acknowledgements

I want to thank Adrian Wright, for always believing in me and for never letting me give up on the idea of writing and publishing a book. I'd also like to thank my family and my wonderful other half, Cody Underwood, for encouraging me to chase my dreams and putting up with all the crazy in the process.

The flowers are all dying
wilting
weeping
fading.

Animals are disappearing,
slaughtered
hunted
used up until there are no more to use.

Oceans are polluted
taken for granted
and treated as if they don't sustain survival.

And we, as humans, are the only ones to blame.

We're malicious. Foul intentions and worse agendas; we destroy our planet, the beautiful goddess that seeks to give us life and happiness, we spit in her face repeatedly; and then we wonder why hurricanes wreck our shores, bury our homes, our children, our loved ones.
We do this to ourselves, so wrapped up in our own malice and greed, we stop focusing on what's important. We stop focusing on each other;

We're left alone, empty, bleeding and bruised.
Trapped with nothing but our secrets and regrets.
We can't live this way forever; there's no time left.

Selfish.
It must run in our blood, buried deep within our DNA.
Rooted in evil, most minds are warped, unable to comprehend emotion, obvious distaste for anything resembling affection.
I've always known that I don't belong here; are there others like me?
Do they feel the air growing heavy?
The shifting of energy in the stars, the atmosphere, mother nature herself.
Panic lives inside me permanently. It has made a special home inside my head, right behind my eyelids. I've made peace with it; welcomed it warmly. Darkness is comforting.
The thunder calms me;
lightning speaks to my soul;
Maybe that's why I always find myself running back to you.

Our tongues used to keep each
other company, now all I want is to
see you rot beneath all of your
misery. We had one hope left, but
neither of us felt like moving. And
somehow, even now, despite all the
hatred and violence, we're drawn to
one another. Like it's our fate to be
destroyed beneath the
weight of our love.
The weight of our lust.
The weight of our lies.

Fire.
Rush.
Run.
The burning sensation in the back of your throat, slowly creeping down your spine, tingling your clit before it makes its way to the soles of your feet...
Yes, that's the rush from polluting your veins with poison. It alters the very essence of your being, often making you lose who you are completely.
I barely fought those demons off and won myself.
And even now, something inside
of me is missing.
Parts of me, pieces of who I was,
Vanished. This anger lives here now, taking over my body. Only a small part of me still exists peacefully. And that part is fighting like hell:

CLAWING.

SCRATCHING.

SCREAMING.

Trying desperately to make her way to the surface.
But the malevolence drags me down; grips my ankles pulling me under, under, under.

I sink.

And I pray that this beast doesn't engulf me.

I only wanted you; but you're gone and I can't get you back.
I keep reaching for the sky,
outstretched
screaming
pleading
I'm begging for you to return to me.
If only time would shift, warp, retreat back to the final moments when your soul left your body; if only you could be saved..
Perhaps then, you could save me and I wouldn't have to live the rest of my life hollowed out and empty.

Your passing was so sudden, shaking me to my core.
I imagine seeing you lying on your deathbed, tubes crammed down your throat.
A machine forcing your lungs to breathe, your heart faintly beating.

I made a choice, a choice to let you die alone.

As your youngest child, I resemble you the most.
You pushed me away, and I disappeared willingly.

If only I would have stayed, if you would have put your narcissistic tendencies aside and been a better mother… I could have been a better daughter.

But I know we both carried the blame; each too prideful to admit it.

Now, I carry the shame; the guilt, the remorse, the burdens of your secrets and mine.
Now, I, alone, am left to deal with the wreckage you left behind inside my mind.

There used to be light, love, hope.
In the deepest cracks within my soul, there used to be dreams of growing old.
The only thing that remains now are cobwebs and malignance.

Turning me into something I tried so desperately not to be….

YOU.

Pieces of me break away,
fall apart,
crumble.

I attempt to pull myself together; trying to claw my way back to the light, to the surface, to the fresh air… but these hands pull me under, drag me down, make me suffer. Amid all this anguish, I keep a small fire burning in my heart. The smoke heats me up, the flames keep me searching for a way out. I won't succumb to these treacherous accusations of treason. I've fought for too long to give up now.

You tell yourself I'm a bastard child, that I mean nothing to no one; you tell yourself I'm weak and I lack good intentions.. but your mind is so clouded by anger and fiction that you don't even see yourself clearly anymore. And I'll admit, I can't see you either. You've become distorted, disfigured and decrepit. You've molted into a thousand faces; and all familiarity is lost.

ABANDONED.

Bloody.
Contusions.
Teeth Marks.
Track Marks.
All at the mercy of…

Forcing me to bend at your will; molding, shaping, breaking me down into whatever you needed me to be; and I let you. Any strength I once had, you stole, like a villain in the night, stalking me. Uttering beautiful, sweet nothings that made me feel safe. I thought I'd found safety in your arms, but the truth is…
I only found my downfall.

His hands are violent.
His eyes are always black.
The pain he inflicts upon me is calculated and cruel. I can't outrun him, no matter how hard I try.

My feet are bloody, my soles are torn and ragged. He's chipping away at my ego, breaking me down until I'm too worn out to stand back up. The fire that used to burn inside of me is fading, growing dim with each day that passes;

His stamina never falters; he never shows even a flicker of weakness, but I know that's because he's feeding off mine. He can see it in my eyes; written all over my body are the stories of his soul.
Deep.
Dark.
Twisted.

He's relentless.

You are unclean; distorted, absent and full of hate.
Foul intentions slip from between your teeth, your tongue dances restlessly behind your lips,
waiting for the perfect moment to strike.
but…
I won't back down; I won't let you destroy me.

Fragile, with my crumbling ego, I cling to you.
You make me whole; there's no going back now.
You're an acrobat dancing through my dreams. My dark
and twisted mind; And I'm an acrobat, dancing on a
tightrope, just hoping to fall into your arms.
Swallow me up, make me yours forever.
I crave the abuse you've always forced upon me,
and now in the aftermath of it all,
I desire you even more.
Stockholm Syndrome at its finest.
I'll always be yours.

The darkness lurking in your eyes, the ice running through your veins, you've hidden away the girl I once was and turned me into this woman who just wants to please you. Constantly in the back of my mind, you're there in the shadows, your voice echoing throughout my body and soul. Part of me searches for a way back to you, but I know I can never go back. You'd destroy everything I have left. So I stay stuck in limbo, hiding these dark desires and pretending that I'm perfectly sane. You've changed me and I don't know who I am anymore without you. So I type these words in hopes that I'll find myself again… Pull the pieces of who I am up out of the dirt, roots and all. I was your flower once…
But now I'm
dead
dying
wilting
weeping
fading into nothing.

You're a leach; sucking me dry; draining me of all my energy... It's exhausting.

The warped way of your nature never leaves me; you've crawled into my brain like a parasite, eating away at every last nerve until there's nothing left.
I've changed. I'm far less patient than the girl I used to be.

Perhaps it's the nightmares;

I'm RUNNING.
Run.
Faster.

My feet are covered in blood, getting cut more and more the faster I flee.
You're chasing me, I hear the leaves crumbling beneath your weight; I search frantically, trying to find anywhere to hide, I have to get away from you.

I spot a shallow alcove to my right; covered with dying flowers and dead trees. I run as fast as I can to the entrance, forcing myself in despite the thorns and poisonous insects all around me. I place my hand over my mouth, close my eyes and try to breathe.

The rustling of leaves that followed closely behind me ceases.

You're here, you're looking for me. Eager to have my blood on your hands.. Footsteps creep closer, you're right outside the small hole I prayed would keep me safe… Suddenly everything falls away, the brush giving me shelter just melts… And now… Your blade is flush with my flesh, ready to end me.

Suddenly, I awake to familiar surroundings. But I quickly realize I'm not safe; your hands are around my throat and once again… I'm looking into the blackest eyes I've ever seen…
I'll never escape you.

And it's times like these; I swear I hear your voice.
You linger so thick in all of my thoughts, I never have a moment of peace.

You play mind games.

Deceitful tricks that warp my perception of reality.
Your feeble attempt to lure me out of hiding.
I try to calm these irrational fears, these unreasonable thoughts,
but all of my coping skills escape me.

You're just as ignorant as you seem.

The terrors haven't left; for a second they remained dormant but they're back tonight with all their teeth out, snarling.

Shaken up doesn't even begin to describe it.
They haunt me. Just like you do and just as my demons always will.

I long for sleep.
I ache for peace.

…but I know I'll never find it.

The fear induced by your hands,
I've always envied your ability, to be so cruel, so violent.
You cease all emotional ties in an instant,
almost as quickly as the anger enters your eyes.

My head is crowded; these voices, these
memories, they never quiet.
They creep in like shadows of the night; hiding,
tormenting me.
Looking for any signs of life.
Opening doors, unlocking windows until they find me.
They always find me.

I'm not sure when I started to finally notice my sanity slipping away. Perhaps it was some time ago, even before I made myself a pin cushion.
I imagine my reality started to shift the day I let your iniquitous ways weave webs around my body.
You crept along, blending in like you belonged there; and I was foolish enough to believe you.
You mastered the art of trickery long before you ever set your sights on me.
You were a chameleon, you always could blend in with the best of them.

Despite having this former history with you, this degrading, sadistic, masochistic history…
I still find myself pacing this fucking room. The more I try to stay still, the more I itch to move.
Longing for you.

Not so much your presence, because picturing your face lights me up with undeniable rage; but the familiar game of cat and mouse. Somewhere along the way, I got accustomed to it;

I reminisce, desperately trying to find a time when I once saw light in your eyes…

But I can't; only terror rests where your soul should be.

The shadows of my insanity are slowly starting to peak around the corners, in the furthest edges of my nightmares, where he slumbers.

I fall to my knees with force, and weakness becomes me.

I've always been a master of running.
Faster than an asteroid, a terrifying death.
I'm pushing and pulling your strings, twisting your reality and crushing your sanity.
Blinded by my beauty, my charisma is charming.
Just call out my name.
I'll hear your cries.

666 is the number of death;
A terrifying demon nestled somewhere in time; a savage monster offering no warnings, no signs. It's judgement day and eventually, we all have to pay.

And as I reach the meeting place… I'm prepared to take my last breath; only it isn't a monster who claims 666… it's you…

And I fear that all the stars in the sky can't save me now.

You fall down.
I fall away…

Dreaming of endless possibilities,
Seeking explanations,
The world always falls silent in my time of need.

I'll never get to see you again.
This energy evaporates.
You're nonexistent.

Careful now.
Watch your step. I'm on a path of self-destruction and I'm coming straight for you.

I began with good intentions,
but the cosmos flipped the script and it's unparalleled.

It was written in the stars all along;

This is my sanity unravelling.

You must think I'm voiceless.
Tell me, do you mind if I steal a heartache? I can't find the harm without you.

Stuck now, I'm trapped in your memories.
So many years have passed and I still can't get those pretty little green eyes out of my head.

Your hands; once so gentle and safe, turned quickly into the sinner you always pretended desperately not to be. You had everyone fooled; hell, you still do and I'd be tongue-tied to think otherwise.

But you see, they don't know you like I do.

SHE doesn't know you like I do.

You always fancied having someone you could control; someone that would bleed if you said cut; I'll admit, that girl was once me, but I began to see through you. And now, you're as transparent as they come.

The ones that love you, the ones you claim to love, they'll always be oblivious.

But the more you try to move on, remember, I'll always be right there… the keeper of the truth; The one who holds all the knowledge of your wrongdoings. You'll never escape me, no matter how far you run, or how fast you flee…

I know you'll always hear my voice in the back of your mind.
I know I'll always be the one you crave to end without mercy.

You hide your intentions behind an endearing smile and a calloused tongue; you'll never amount to anything if you stay on this path. I used to take your threats as weightless, pathetic attempts to strike fear into my being.

But now I'm not so sure. My palms sweat when I think of your monstrous ways. The possibility of what you may actually be capable of stops me dead in my tracks. Who are you, who have you become?

You're not the man I once knew; or perhaps you were and I was always too blinded by your beauty to see it.

I can't shake this feeling that he's after me; plotting, pretending, portraying to love me… When all he really wants to do is dismember my soul, my body, my integrity.

You rip away at me; my heart, my clothes, my everything. I tried saying no, I screamed, and begged for mercy. But you're as cold hearted as they come. You shoved my face deeper into the pillows, as you shoved yourself deeper inside me. Your words ring in my ears, as clearly as the tears run down my cheeks remembering what you did to me.

ABUSED.

Finding my way back from the echoes of my past;
You used to be a part of me. You used to control every move I made, every thought that entered my brain was consumed by you. But I've regained control and I'm done playing the victim.

You taught me many things, and now I know…

how to be a wolf in sheep's clothing.

In the treeline, there; I can see it.
Him?
Her?

An apparition.

Is it you or am I dreaming? Stuck in purgatory, I keep
reaching for you. But you never outstretch your hands;
you refuse me, just as I've always refused you.
You always said that I was meant for more than this, more
than this place, more than this suffering.
Your voice used to ring so clearly in my ears; I could hear
you as clearly as the muffled sound of screaming that I
hear now.

Where have you disappeared to?
It's dark.
It's cold.
I no longer feel you here with me.

Hunt.
Watch.
Track.
Stalk.

What if the reason we always feel watched,
is because the ones who leave us,
linger here.
All around us. Invisible. Isolated.

We can't hear them.
We can't see them.
but they're there…
Always just barely escaping us.

Your eyes; so green…
like the deep lagoons of a long-lost sea.
I've spent so long searching for you; and suddenly you come in like a hurricane.

DESTRUCTION.

Chills; they line my legs and your blood lines my walls.
I never would have thought such chaos would come of this.

REVENGE.

The streetlights faintly light the rundown streets, barely putting out enough lumens to see that we've all been betrayed.
The fog makes the anticipation worse; the anticipation of knowing soon, we'll be fighting a war we can never win.
Camouflaged; brilliantly disguising themselves as normal, masquerading like they belong here.
Enemies will always be around us.
Secretly. Silently. Snake-like. Lurking.

There are many different forms of deception; the art of trickery.
Many different styles of manipulation and a vast array of methods to master them.

My brain never ceases at a crossroads; I've always been one to stay on my toes.

Questions; so many questions.

I take note of your small, subtle movements.
The direction of your gaze points directly back at me.
The curiosity sits heavily atop your eyebrows, causing them to crease with inspection.
Anxiously waiting to spout my secrets, you always loved making a mockery of me.

Consistently. Constantly. Continuously.
You reach out your hands, holding onto endless hope that I'll grab you at the last second and pull you up out of this grave you've been digging.

But you collapse deeper into the dirt, falling just out of reach.
I embrace the grass stains left on my jeans as a gentle reminder of your memory.

I tried, I really tried desperately to bring you back to the surface, but the weight of all your burdens was just too heavy… Please don't fail me now.

Lucid dreaming; panic rises.
My hands grow numb, my fingernails are bloody and bleeding.
I give up.

I find my composure tucked neatly away inside the spot where my empathy used to be; pull yourself together…
I've had enough.

It's time to let go of these pieces of us.